T0353752

The Day I Shook David Bowies hand

and other Stories of Life on the Road

By Andrew Mian

AuthorHouse™ UK
1663 Liberty Drive
Bloomington, IN 47403 USA
www.authorhouse.co.uk
UK TFN: 0800 0148641 (Toll Free inside the UK)
UK Local: 02036 956322 (+44 20 3695 6322 from outside the UK)

Because of the dynamic nature of the Internet, any web addresses or links contained in this book may have changed since publication and may no longer be valid. The views expressed in this work are solely those of the author and do not necessarily reflect the views of the publisher, and the publisher hereby disclaims any responsibility for them.

Any people depicted in stock imagery provided by Getty Images are models, and such images are being used for illustrative purposes only.
Certain stock imagery © Getty Images.

This book is printed on acid-free paper.

ISBN: 979-8-8230-9106-0 (sc)
ISBN: 979-8-8230-9105-3 (e)

Print information available on the last page.

Published by AuthorHouse 02/11/2025

authorHOUSE®

The Day I Shook David Bowies hand

and other Stories of

Life on the Road

Tom Robinson Band April 1979

The Tom Robinson Band was my first ever concert at The Queenway in 1979

I must admit I do not remember much about this concert but it was my first introduction to live music.

My second concert holds many more memories

Led Zeppelin August 1979

The grounds of Knebworth House near the village of Knebworth had been a major venue for open air rock and pop concerts since 1974. In 1979, veteran promoter Freddy Bannister booked Led Zeppelin to play that year's concerts which took place on 4 August[1] and 11 August[2] after the bandleader of the Electric Light Orchestra, Jeff Lynne, turned down the offer to headline the festival.

Led Zeppelin had not performed live for two years, since the death of Robert Plant's son during the band's 1977 North American tour, and they had not performed in the United Kingdom for four years. Their manager Peter Grant decided that the band should perform at Knebworth instead of embarking on a lengthy tour.

In 1979 the tickets were £7.50 an excessive price for a 17 yeard old. Luckily my parents gave me the money and three friends and I set off by Coach to Knebworth

We arrived at approximately 1pm on the 11th August, the day before the event. We had little money so we spent time looking around Knebworth before deciding to sleep in the coach station that night. Luckily it was August and quite warm but we did not get much sleep that night.

The next day at 8am we made our way the the festival site. Were we the first ? not by a long shot. Thousands of peiople were in the queue before us

At about 10am we entered the arena, which was huge. The first band on was Fairport Convention folliowed by Chas and Dave, The Marshall Tucker Band, Southside Johnny and the Ashbury Dukes, Todd Rungren and Utopia and The New Barbarians

We found out later thar over 200,000 people attended that event. The music was great but certain stiuations were less than desirable. For example going to the toilet. It was impossible for anyone to go to the toilet and later meet up with their friends, so people ended up urinating where they stood.

The time then came for Led Zeppelin to take the stage. For many of us this was out first time seeing this amazing group (and subsequantly one of the last because drummer John Bonham died 25 September 1980)

Zep took to the stage as the sun was setting, keeping everyone waiting for what felt like ages. When they did arrive the sound was terrible for about the first half an hour, swirling around and fading in and out. As the subsequent film well illustrates, the band are on top form, allowing for the usual sloppy playing by Page. I loved Achilles Last Stand, to me that's when they were at their most majestic and unique. I remember feeling that at that time.

An amazing concert from one of the worlds best bands

Later in 1979 and 1980 I attended probably the best concerts if my life. Peter Gabriel and Genesis appearead at The Friars Rock Club in Aylesbury.

Peter Gabriel August 1979

Gabriel had a long history of appearing at Friars with his old band Genesis. On Saturday June 19th 1971, Peter decided to jump into the audience but at the crucial moment people changed direction and Peter landed badly on the floor. Peter limped back to finish the set and it was not until later that he was told he had broken his leg.n n

At this concert on Friday August 30th 1979 much to peoples surprise Phil Collins joined him on drums. This time Peter did not jump into the audience but he did walk through tPeter Gabriel is and always will be a Friars hero. After 1979, he continued to go from strength to strength as a solo artiste, along the way producing some unforgettable material such as the haunting "Biko" and the video legend that is "Sledgehammer" (although these are not his best works in our humble opinion). His productivity on record at least has not been quick, but this is tempered with the other good works that he does with other artistes (check out Paula Cole for example), Womad etc. He is arguably more responsible for the wider acceptance of world music in this country than any other artiste. He also helped develop the music downloading systems we take as second nature today. He briefly reunited with Genesis in 1982 to raise money for Womad and declined the offer to reform with Genesis in 2007 although he apparently hasn't completely ruled it out. He played UK dates with an orchestra in 2011 and continues to do that in 2012. in 2013 he brings his so tour to the crowd

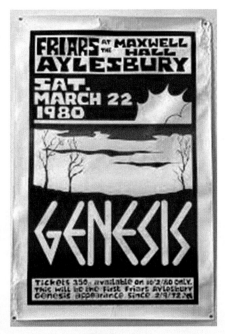

GENESIS

My signed ticket from the night

Genesis are an English rock band formed at Charterhouse School, Godalming, Surrey, in 1967. The band's most commercially successful line-up consists of keyboardist Tony Banks, bassist/guitarist Mike Rutherford and drummer/singer Phil Collins. The 1970s line-up featuring singer Peter Gabriel and guitarist Steve Hackett was among the pioneers of progressive rock.

The group were formed by five Charterhouse pupils, including Banks, Rutherford, Gabriel, and Anthony Phillips, and named by former Charterhouse pupil Jonathan King, who arranged for them to record several singles and their debut album From Genesis to Revelation in 1968. After splitting from King, the band began touring, signed with Charisma Records and became a progressive rock band on Trespass (1970). Following Phillips' departure, Genesis recruited Collins and

Hackett and recorded Nursery Cryme (1971). Their live shows began to feature Gabriel's theatrical costumes and performances. Foxtrot (1972) was their first hit in the UK and Selling England by the

Pound (1973) reached number three there, featuring their first UK hit "I Know What I Like (In Your Wardrobe)". The concept album The Lamb Lies Down on Broadway (1974) was promoted with a transatlantic tour and an elaborate stage show, before Gabriel left the group.

Collins took over as lead singer, and the group released A Trick of the Tail and Wind & Wuthering (both 1976) with continued success. Hackett left Genesis in 1977, reducing the band to Banks, Rutherford, and Collins. Their ninth studio album, ... And Then There Were Three ... (1978), contained the band's first major hit "Follow You Follow Me". Their next five albums – Duke (1980), Abacab (1981), Genesis (1983), Invisible Touch (1986) and We Can't Dance (1991) – were also successful. Collins left Genesis in 1996, and Banks and Rutherford replaced him with Ray Wilson, who appeared on their final album Calling All Stations (1997). The commercial failure of the album led to a group hiatus. Banks, Rutherford and Collins reunited for the Turn It On Again Tour in 2007, and again in 2021 for The Last Domino? Tour.

With between 100 million and 150 million albums sold worldwide, Genesis are one of the world's best-selling music artists. Their discography includes 15 studio and six live albums. They have won numerous awards (including a Grammy Award for Best Concept Music Video with "Land of Confusion") and have inspired a number of tribute bands recreating Genesis shows from various stages of the band's career. In 2010, Genesis were inducted into the Rock and Roll Hall of Fame.

A few montha later Genesis announced they would also be appearing at Friars. Six weeks previous to the show myself and hunderd others queued up all night to get tickets in the local cattle market,. . It was a long cold night in February but Friars kept up warm with continuous music and even porridge in the morning served from a wheelbarrow

The concert itseld was amazing. Genesis were used to performing in large stadiums and Friars Aylesbury held only 1200. They broufght the full London show for Friars who had to extend their stage for the concert. "The moments that Friars dreamt of. Having spent time queuing in the cattle market six weeks previously, the moment came around when what was then starting to become one of the world's biggest bands took to the boards at Aylesbury. Promoting the Duke album they stormed through classics from the previous 10 years. Phil Collins was on good form too. David Stopps presented the band with the Talent Winners Cup and a dossier/file of the names of all those who had queued up in the cattle market. So one of them has my name somewhere ... A great gig."

My first promotion
Whippersnapper

It was after these concerts that I got into my mind that I would like to promote a concert.

I chose the 400 capacity Leighton Buzzard Library Theatre as my venue. I then approached Dave Pegg from the band Fairport Convention to see if he could help me with a band. He replied thast he was sorry but his band was busy on the date I had chosen but to contact an ex Fairport member, Dave Swarbrick to see if he could help. Dave replied that he was available with his band Whippernanapper.

Whippersnapper consister of Dave Swarbrick, Chris Leslie,who later joined Fairport Convention, Kevin Dempsey and Martin Jenkins. I took photos of the event including a great shot of Dave Swarbrick and Chris Leslie fighting with fiddles. A story of this photo will appear later in this story.

The concert was a mild success. A friend helped me with the lights and we did not make a loss. One of the highligts was me introducing the supoport act, Simon and Andrew Loake. Now being only 5'4" Andrew towered over me by being nearly 6 foot. However when Simon took to the stage his 6 foot 6 made the audience laugh. I introduced the band, told a short joke, the audience laughed and the concert was up and running

Whippersnapper was an English folk band formed in 1980, consisting of Dave Swarbrick (fiddle, mandolin, vocals), Chris Leslie (fiddle, mandolin, vocals), Kevin Dempsey (guitar, vocals) and Martin Jenkins (mando-cello, flute, vocals).

Swarbrick left the group in 1989, and the band continued as a trio until 1993, with the only album recorded that line-up being Stories. During that time, Dempsey and Leslie released an album called Always With You as a duo. The band split when Jenkins left the group in 1993. However, they did tour briefly again in 1994.

Following Swarbrick's recovery from illness, Whippersnapper toured again as a full four piece in both 2008 and 2009. Martin Jenkins (born 17 July 1946, London, England) died on 17 May 2011, in Sofia, Bulgaria, from a heart attack. Not to be confused with the Australian indie rock group, The Whipper Snappers, who coincidentally played during the period 1988 to 1993.ning.

This takes me back to the carpet shop where I was writing letters to promoters and Record Companies looking for a job. Weeks later I had received two replies. One from Dave Pegg saying sorry but he knew on nothing suitable at the time. The other was from Beth Berman who was

Harvey Goldsmiths manager. She invited me to London for an interview.

1979 Glastonbury

Glastonbury Festival (formally Glastonbury Festival of Contemporary Performing Arts) is a five-day festival of contemporary performing arts that takes place in Pilton, Somerset, in England. In addition to contemporary music, the festival hosts dance, comedy, theatre, circus, cabaret, and other arts. Leading pop and rock artists have headlined, alongside thousands of others appearing on smaller stages and performance areas. Films and albums recorded at Glastonbury have been released, and the festival receives extensive television and newspaper coverage. Glastonbury is attended by around 200,000 people,[2] requiring extensive infrastructure in terms of security, transport, water, and electricity supply. The majority of staff are volunteers, helping the festival to raise millions of pounds for charity organisations.[3]

Regarded as a major event in British culture, the festival is inspired by the ethos of the hippie, counterculture, and free festival movements. It retains vestiges of these traditions, such as the Green Fields area, which includes sections known as the Green Futures and Healing Field.[4] After the 1970s, the festival took place almost every year and grew in size, with the number of attendees sometimes being swollen by gatecrashers. Michael Eavis hosted the first festival, then called Pilton Festival, after seeing an open-air Led Zeppelin concert at the 1970 Bath Festival of Blues and Progressive Music. The festival's record crowd is 300,000 people, set at the 1994 festival, when headliners the Levellers performed a set on The Pyramid Stage

Glastonbury Festival was held intermittently from 1970 until 1981. Since then, it has been held most years, except for "fallow years" taken mostly at five-year intervals, intended to give the land, local population, and organisers a break. 2018 was a "fallow year" and the following festival took place from 26 to 30 June 2019.[6] Glastonbury has had two consecutive "fallow years" since the last festival took place in 2019 due to the COVID-19 pandemic.[7](WIKAPEDIA)

Before the interview, I went to my first Glastonbury. I mainly went to see Peter Gabriel but it was an amazing event.Now a three dayfestival and was still referred to as the Glastonbury Fayre but with the theme of "the year of the child". Bill Harkin and Arabella Churchill were the instigators on this occasion and turned to Michael Eavis for financial backing. He secured a bank loan against the deeds of the farm. Special provision and entertainment was provided for children and it was at this event that the concept of the Children's World charity was born which still exists today and works in special schools throughout Somerset and Avon Again, despite the numbers attending, the organisers suffered a huge financial loss and no one wanted to risk another festival in 1980. It was also this summer that Michael's youngest daughter, Emily was born.

Acts included: Peter Gabriel, Steve Hillage, Alex Harvey Band, Sky and the Footsbarn Theatre. Attendance: 12,000. Tickets: £5.

Glastonbury Festival is the largest greenfield music and performing arts festival in the world and a template for all the festivals that have come after it. The difference is that Glastonbury has all the best aspects of being at a festival in one astonishing bundle.

It's like going to another country; a thrilling and vibrant cultural meltingpot and inspirational Brigadoon that appears every year or so. Coming to Glastonbury involves a fair amount of travel, and probably a queue to get in but, when you get past these impediments, you enter a huge tented city, a mini-state under canvas. British law still applies, but the rules of society are a bit different, a little bit freer. Everyone is here to have a wild time in their own way.

The Festival takes place in a beautiful location – 900 acres in the Vale of Avalon, an area steeped in symbolism, mythology and religious traditions dating back many hundreds of years. It's where King Arthur may be buried, where Joseph of Arimathea is said to have walked, where ley lines converge. And the site is ENORMOUS – more than a mile and a half across, with a perimeter of about eight and a half miles.

Then there are the people; thousands of them in all their astonishing and splendid diversity! There is only one common characteristic of a Glastonbury-goer – they understand that Glastonbury Festival offers them more opportunity than any other happening to have the best weekend of the year or even of a life-time, and they are determined to have it! You'll meet all kinds of people, of all ages, backgrounds, nationalities, lifestyles, faiths, concepts of fashion (or lack of it) and musical taste. Some will undoubtedly wear silly hats or buy shirts that they'll never wear again … until next year, that is. The overall vibe of the Festival is consistently mellow and friendly, even in the event of rain and all that comes with rain, a field and thousands upon thousands of tramping feet.

There will be moments when you ask yourself the inevitable: "Why can't life always be like this?" There will be enlightenments, awakenings, surreal happenings, Damascene epiphanies and people doing the strangest things in public. Sometimes the strangest things you'll see happening have been booked well in advance – but often it will be people spontaneously reacting to the spirit of the Festival. No two people's Festival experience will be the same unless they're tied together, in which case they're probably part of a theatre compa

In 1979 it was easy to walk around Glastonbuty with just 12,000 people. I went to Glastonbury every year until 1999. I saw some amazing acts and had a great time. However in 1999 I went to my last Glastonbury. The reason for this is that I mainly wanted to see REM. Unfortunately so did most of the crowd which had risen from 12,500 to over 100,000. In 1999 I was walking from one field to another to see REM. Unfortunately, as ealier said. so were many other people.

At one point it was so dangerouns I felt in danger of getting crushed.

I decided to turn back and miss REM. Glastonbury has grown even larger. In 2019 175,000 people attended but for me 1999 was enough.

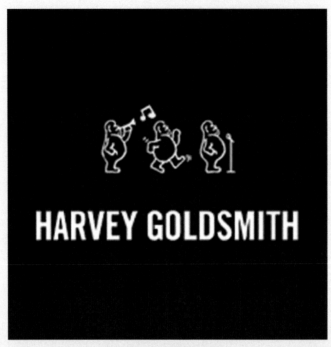

Harvey Goldsmith

Harvey Goldsmith CBE (born 4 March 1946 in Edgware, Middlesex) is an English performing arts promoter. He is best known as a promoter of rock concerts, charity concerts, television broadcasts for the Prince's Trust and more recently the Teenage Cancer Trust shows at the Royal Albert Hall.

In 1985, Goldsmith promoted the Live Aid concert held at Wembley Stadium in London.[1] During early 2007, he appeared on the Channel 4 programme Get Your Act Together with Harvey Goldsmith. In October the same year, he promoted a reunion concert for surviving members of Led Zeppelin in memory of Atlantic Records founder Ahmet Ertegun, which was held at London's O2 Arena.

Goldsmith has produced, managed and promoted shows with many of the world's major artists including Yes, Genesis, Led Zeppelin, Pink Floyd, Queen, The Eagles, Elton John, U2, Madonna, Andrea Bocelli, Muse, Bob Dylan, The Rolling Stones, The Who, Bruce Springsteen, Santana, Luciano Pavarotti, Sheryl Crow, Shania Twain, Bee Gees, Jools Holland, Oasis, Paul Weller, Rod Stewart, Diana Ross, Saxon, Shirley Bassey, Coldplay, Nigel Kennedy, Eric Clapton, Richard Ashcroft, Ash,

Madness, Aswad, David Gray, Scissor Sisters, Van Morrison, Sting, and Jeff Beck.[2][3]th

Early in 1982 I attended the interview and it was for the job of messenger. I was to deliver inportant letters to other promoters and managers in and around Oxford Street . I immediately said yes and started work the following Monday. I was to receive £45 per week cash in hand. This might not seem a lot but in 1981 a train ticket from Leighton Buzzard to Oxford Srteet was only £3. Times that by 5 days + = £15 so I had more than enough money to keep me going.

The staff at Harvey Goldsmith Entertainments (HGE) were quite interesting and you might think being a messenger was a boring role but you would be mistaken.

I got to meet a lot of interesting people. One of these was Prince Rupert Lowensten who was The Rolling Stones finalcial manager with an office just off Regent Street. He was very chatty and told me a lot of stories the Rolling Stones.

Another was Robert Stigwood who was Eric Claton's manager. Not only was he very easy to talk to but after a few meetings he gave me a ticket to and upcoming Eric show at Wembley

Finally I got to meet Lynsdey de Paul. She was looking lost around Oxford Street. I knew she had an aoopintment with Hayver so Iapproached her. At first she probably thought I was just a fan looking for an autograph but when I told her I worked for HGE she followed me up to his office where she gratefully said thank you before I went on my way

After a year of being a messenger I approached HGE main promoter, a man called Andrew Zewck. I told him that although I didnt mind being a messenger I wanted to do more for the company. He said to wait a few days and he would ask Harvey.

A couple of days went by and he told me he would like to make me an assistant promoter. Litttle did I know that most if not all of the other staff were assistant promoters. I did mean a payrise unto to £50.

I did ask Andrew what this promotion meant. He basically said I had to accomapny him to all events and do as he asked. (This later changed) For the first few weeks nothing changed. There were no shows on so I resorted to my life as a messenger.

Hand picked by Billy.

Billy Connolly

Billy Connolly

However, all this changed when a large Scotsman entered the office

Little did I know but HGE also promoted Billy Connolly.

Billy was an amazing man who was funny all the time. We chatted and seemed to get on Ok.

It was then that Andrew Zweck asked me if I would like to go on tour with Billy. YES was the asnswer. My job was to accompany Billy and his roadie friend Jamie to a number of UK Concerts. My job was to do basically any thing Billy asked. I packed my bags and was ready to go on tour late 1981

The tour consisted of dates at:

The Theatre Royal Plymouth

Pavilion Theatre Bounemouth

Odeon Theatre Ayr, Scotland

De Montfot Hall Leicester

Hammersmith Odeon 3 shows

The first night at Brighton set the scene for all the other shows. We arrived in Brighton at approximately 1pm. We were all staying at a local Premier Inn. Most bands on tour had a rider which is a list of things they require in their dressing room on a nightly basis. Now Billy was a very easy going chap with little requests. At this time Billy was drinking (he later gave up) and his main request was a bottle of Whisky in his room every night. He didn't really mind what Whiskey but he preferred Famous Gouse. This was easily obtainable throughout the UK. Now Billy has aways said he does not write things down when doing a show. He just gets onto the stage and starts talking abought things that might have happened either recetenly or in his past. I have no idea how he did it but he had the audience in stitches every night.

The eight shows I saw on the tour were never the same. There was a general theme but his dialogue was constantly changing. One amazing thing about Billy is that aside from the Whisky he required nothing else on his room. Every night Billy, Jamie and myself would go out for a meal at a local eaterie. Were were just three chaps entering a restaurant looking for something to eat. On occasion the host would show to a table and might recognise Billy but nothing was ever said.

Now these eateries were nothing special. Somtimes there were just restaurants adjoining a pub. Other times they migt be something slightly more special but it was never anything too expensive. And believe it or not, although he was quite well known at the time Billy was only approached twice for an autograph.

Other things I had to do for Billy was occasionally get his trousers cleaned, buy him cigarettes and generally make sure he was OK

Later on in my time for HGE I was to work with and meet some superstars But I must admit that my time with Billy has by far my favourite. One final story. When in 1983 I decided to leave HGE Billy signed a phoo for me. I will never forget what he wrote

"To Andrew, whose leaving has me in floods of tears. Who Am i going to bully now. The girls are all too big Billy."

The Billy tour was late December 1981 and after the tour I took a weeks annual leave and stayed at home. I was living with my parents at the time. Christmas came and went and very soon it was 1982. The first few months of 1982 were quite boring. There was some messenger work to be done but mainly we spent time in the office chatting and waiting for the next concert.

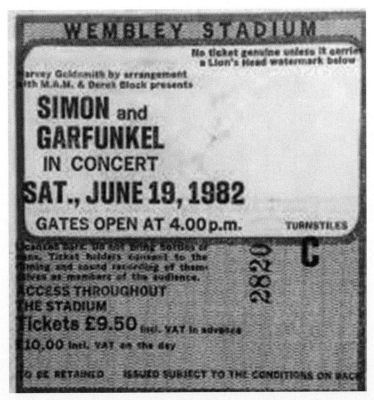

Simon and Garfunkel June 1982

Simon & Garfunkel were an American folk-rock duo consisting of singer-songwriter Paul Simon and singer Art Garfunkel. They were one of the best-selling music groups of the 1960s, and their biggest hits—including "The Sound of Silence" (1965), "Mrs. Robinson" (1968), "The Boxer"

(1969), and "Bridge over Troubled Water" (1970)—reached number one on singles charts worldwide.

Simon and Garfunkel met in elementary school in Queens, New York, in 1953, where they learned to harmonize together and began writing material. By 1957, under the name Tom & Jerry, the teenagers had their first minor success with "Hey Schoolgirl", a song imitating their idols the Everly Brothers. In 1963, aware of a growing public interest in folk music, they regrouped and were signed to Columbia Records as Simon & Garfunkel. Their debut, Wednesday Morning, 3 A.M., sold poorly, and they once again disbanded; Simon returned to a solo career, this time in England. In

June 1965, a new version of "The Sound of Silence" overdubbed with electric guitar and drums became a major U.S. AM radio hit, reaching number one on the Billboard Hot 100. The duo reunited to release a second studio album, Sounds of Silence, and tour colleges nationwide. On their third release, Parsley, Sage, Rosemary and Thyme (1966), the duo assumed more creative control. Their music was featured in the 1967 film The Graduate, giving them further exposure. Their next album Bookends (1968) topped the Billboard 200 chart[2] and included the number-one single "Mrs. Robinson" from the film.

The duo's often rocky relationship led to artistic disagreements and their breakup in 1970. Their final studio album, Bridge over Troubled Water, was released in January of that year, becoming their most successful release and one of the world's best-selling albums. After their breakup, Simon released a number of acclaimed albums, including

1986's Graceland.[3] Garfunkel released solo hits such as "All I Know" and briefly pursued an acting career, with leading roles in two Mike Nichols films, Catch-22 and Carnal Knowledge, and in Nicolas Roeg's 1980 Bad Timing. The duo have reunited several times, most famously in 1981 for The Concert in Central Park, which attracted more than 500,000 people, one of the largest concert attendances in history.[4]

Simon & Garfunkel won 10 Grammy Awards and were inducted into the Rock and Roll Hall of Fame in 1990.[5] Rolling Stone ranked them number 3 on its list of the 20 Greatest Duos of All Time.[6] Richie Unterberger described them as "the most successful folk-rock duo of the 1960s" and one of the most popular artists from the decade.[1] They are among the best-selling music artists, having sold more than 100 million records.[7] Bridge over Troubled Water is ranked at number 172 on Rolling Stone's 500 Greatest Albums of All Time.[8](WIKAPEDIA)

It wasn't until February that things began to get very interesting. It was announced That HGE were going to put on Simon and Garfunkel at Wembley Stadium and a Rolling Stones tour My initial job along with many others was to open mail and send out tickets as requested. A great point about this was that I got paid 20p for every ticket I sent out. I usually did approximately 500 tickets a day. Work it out. On top of my £50 a week I was making £100 a day selling tickets. By the end of May when the tickets for both shows were sold out I was in my eyes, a rich man. The actual concert was on Saturday June 19 1982

My job a week before the concert was to study the riders and purchase any items on it. As it was only one concert the rider wasn't huge but I do remember Paul Simon requesting a bottle of Jack Daniels, a Meat loaf meal before the show and vegetarian sandwiches after the show.

Art Garfunkel requested a home made burger before the show, a bottle of Belvedere Vodka and falafels after the show. Part of my job was to visit the Wembley chef who kindly told me that he could provide the meals but that I would have to purchase the drinks.

Jack Daniels was easy but I had to go to Fortnum and Masons for the Belvedere Vodka. This was a very easy rider to accomodate. Let me give you example of riders that can range from tame to ridiculous. In 2017 Ed Sheerhan played Glastonbury Festival. Hs rider was some Robinson squash, a six pack of coca cola, a six pack of Fanta Orange, a six pack of Sprite and a jar of Manuka honey. The total cost amounts to less than £60

On the other hand when Maria Carery switched on the christmas lights at Westfield shopping centre she requested 100 doves and 20 kittens. What the doves and kittens were for I'll never know but the kittens could not be arranged due to health and safety issues.

The day arrived and all was readyI was lucky enough to have to introduce the chef to both artists. I remember Paul being in a great mood but Art was more withdrawn.

It was not until after the show I was told that Simon and Garfunkel did not like each other. On stage they were consumate professionals but off the stage nothing. Why then did they work together I asked. I was then told. Wembley holds 82,000 and tickets were an average £8 to

£10. So at £9 x 82,000 equals £738,000. Now putting on the show obviously cost money but I reackon at the end of the day both Paul and Art made approximately £150,000. For a two hour show that equates to £75,000 an hour.

Princes Trust

The Prince's Trust is a charity in the United Kingdom founded in 1976 by Charles, Prince of Wales, to help vulnerable young people get their lives on track. It supports 11 to 30-year-olds who are unemployed and those struggling at school and at risk of exclusion. Many of the young people helped by The Trust are in or leaving care, facing issues such as homelessness or mental health problems, or have been in trouble with the law.

It runs a range of training programmes, providing practical and financial support to build young people's confidence and motivation. Each year they work with about 60,000 young people; with three in four moving on to employment, education, volunteering or training.

In 1999, the numerous Trust charities were brought together as The Prince's Trust and was acknowledged by The Queen at a ceremony in Buckingham Palace where she granted it a Royal Charter. The following year it devolved in Wales, Scotland, Northern Ireland and other English regions but overall control remained in London. The Prince's Trust fundraising and campaign events are often hosted and feature

entertainers from around the world. In April 2011 the youth charity Fairbridge became part of the Trust. [3] In 2015, Prince's Trust International was launched to collaborate with other charities and organisations in other countries (mostly Commonwealth nations) to help young people in those countries.[4]

The Prince's Trust is one of the most successful funding organisations in the UK and the UK's leading youth charity, having helped over 950,000 young people turn their lives around,[5][6] created 125,000 entrepreneurs and given business support to 395,000 people in the UK.[7] From 2006 to 2016, its work for the youth has been worth an estimated £1.4 billion.[In July 1082 Harvery promoted a Princes Trust Concert. Performers (in alphabetical order): Joan Armatrading Gary Brooker (Procul Harum) Kate Bush Phil Collins Jethro Tull Mick Karn (Japan) Madness Robert Plant Pete Townshend (The Who) Unity Midge Ure

I had a baqckstage pass for this concert which was attended by Prince Charles and Lady Diane. Although I saw both of them I was to scruffy to be introduced.

There are a couple of special moments thast I remember from that show. Firstly, sometime during the concert I went to the toilet and found myself urinating next to Pete Townsend. No words were exchanged (why would we) and we both went our seperate ways. But I later thought to myself, I shared a urinal with Pete Townsend. Wow!

Later on in the show Kate Bush was performing. She performed a number of her hits as I watched stage left. During one of her songs I noticed that one of he dress strands had come loose. Do you believe I was brave enough to enter the stage and fix her dress. Of course, I wasn't another member of the crew did But it COULD have been me, if I was a bit braver.

The Rolling Stones

The Rolling Stones are an English rock band formed in London in 1962. Diverging from the pop rock of the early-1960s, the Rolling Stones pioneered the gritty, heavier-driven sound that came to define hard rock.[1] Their first stable line-up was vocalist Mick Jagger, multi-instrumentalist Brian Jones, guitarist Keith Richards, drummer Charlie Watts, and bassist Bill Wyman. During their formative years Brian Jones was the primary leader: he put the band together, named it, and drove the sound and look of the band. After Andrew Loog Oldham became the group's manager in 1963, he encouraged them to write their own songs. Jagger and Richards became the primary creative force behind the band, alienating Jones, who developed a drug addiction that interfered with his ability to meaningfully contribute. He left the band shortly before his death in 1969, having been replaced by guitarist Mick Taylor, who in turn left in 1974 to be replaced by Ronnie Wood. Since

Wyman's departure in 1993, the band has continued with a four-piece core, with Darryl Jones playing bass on tour and on most studio recordings.

Rooted in blues and early rock and roll, the Rolling Stones started out playing covers and were at the forefront of the British Invasion in 1964, also being identified with the youthful and rebellious counterculture of the 1960s. They then found greater success with their own material as "(I Can't Get No) Satisfaction", "Get Off of My Cloud" and "Paint It Black" became No. 1 hits in the UK, North America, Australia and Europe. Aftermath (1966) – their first entirely original album – is considered the most important of their formative records.[2] In 1967, they had the double-sided hit "Ruby Tuesday"/"Let's Spend the Night Together" and then experimented with psychedelic rock on Their Satanic Majesties Request. They went back to their roots with such hits as "Jumpin' Jack Flash" (1968) and "Honky Tonk Women" (1969), and albums such as Beggars Banquet (1968), featuring "Sympathy for the Devil", and Let It Bleed (1969), featuring "You Can't Always Get What You Want" and "Gimme Shelter". Let It Bleed was the first of five straight No. 1 albums in the UK. In 1969, they were first introduced on stage as 'The Greatest Rock and Roll Band in the World'.

Sticky Fingers (1971), which yielded "Brown Sugar", was the first of eight consecutive No. 1 studio albums in the US for the Rolling Stones. Exile on Main St. (1972), featuring "Tumbling Dice", and Goats Head Soup (1973), yielding the hit ballad "Angie", were also best sellers. They released successful albums until the early 1980s, including thei

argest sellers: Some Girls (1978), featuring the disco-tinged "Miss You"; and Tattoo You (1981), featuring the hit rocker "Start Me Up". They then kept a low profile until 1989 when they released Steel Wheels, featuring "Mixed Emotions", which was followed by Voodoo Lounge (1994), a worldwide number one album that yielded the popular "Love Is Strong". Both albums were promoted by large stadium and arena tours as the Stones continue to be a huge concert attraction; by 2007 they had four of the top five highest-grossing concert tours of all time. Their latest album, Blue & Lonesome (2016), became their twelfth UK number-one album. Their No Filter Tour ran for two years concluding in August 2019. They have released 30 studio albums, 23 live albums, and numerous compilations.

The Rolling Stones' estimated record sales of 240 million makes them one of the best-selling music artists of all time. The band has won three Grammy Awards and a Grammy Lifetime Achievement Award. They were inducted into the Rock and Roll Hall of Fame in 1989 and the UK Music Hall of Fame in 2004. In 2008, the Rolling Stones were listed 10th on the Billboard Hot 100 All-Time Top Artists chart, and in 2019 Billboard magazine ranked them second in their list of the "Greatest Artists of All Time" based on US chart success.[3] They are ranked fourth on Rolling Stone's list of the Greatest Artists of All Time.[4](WIKAPEDIA)

In early 1982 The Rolling Stones announced their "Tattoo You" tour dates. I was not involved in their shows at Glasgow, Aberdeen or Edinburgh because these were done by another promoter but there were to be two shows in London at Wembley Stadium on 25 June 1982 and a special warm up show at the 100 Club in Oxford Street a month earlier

I was lucky enough with 300 others to see the Stones at the 100 Club. his was an incredile chance to see the Stones close up. They performed all their hits and put on an amazing show. Now I know i have told you all bout riders before but the Rolling Stones Rider was something to be seen. It ran to 15 pages

It would take too much space the incude it all here but bear with me and Ill give you a brief outine. (sorry it will not be brief)

Page 1 and 2 was what rooms they needed at each venue. They were to have a Workout Room, A Tuning Room, and up to 3 dressing rooms.

In addition to thsese rooms the required two (2) smartly dressed, well groomed hostesses to assist serving food to the band at 3pm on the fay of the show. Table waiting experience preferred.

Page 3 was all 2bout flowers. The Stones required:-

- Two White Casablanca Lily arrangement with weeping Eucalyptus, deliverd in a vase.
- Two White Casablaca Lillieas arrangements with White fresia, deliverd in a vase
- One Long stemmesd White rose with Fressia arrangements in a vase
- Four dozen long stem White Roses with White Fewssia arrangement in a Vase

Page 4 was all abit what cars they needed. The rider states

- Vans and drivers will be required to transport personellto and from the hotels from the first build sayto the completion of the removal of the stage. Many times this will require the vans to be used continuously for 18 hours or more
- During the production loasd in and performance day we will require a total of two passenger vans and two drivers for the production crew· one quality town car with drives i.e. Lincoln, Mercedes, BMW will be required for the Rolling Stones band members. Thses cars must have dark tinted windows, they must not be white and they must not be a limousine

The next few pages were raken up with more technical requests so I not got to bore you until I come to the page that I had to purchase. This was the list for 3 dressing rooms

- Trash Can lined with trash bag
- Plates, Bowls, Napkins, Knives, Forks, Spoons, Wine glasses, Hot Cup and 1 package of plastic 16oz cups (500ml) to cater for 20 people
- I bottle opener
- 1 Corkscrew
- ! botle of Tobasco Hot Sauce
- 1 box of matches (Very Important)
- 1 sharp metal knife and cut1ting board
- 1 case (24 bottles) Alkline Water
- 1 case (24 bottles) of Still Water (No Evian/ Nestle/ Dasani/Aquafina)
- 4 cand Red Bull
- 1 large bottle of Pomegranate Juice
- 1 Large bottle Silver Patron Tequila

- 1 Large bottle Kettle One Vodka
- 12 bottles of Stella
- 12 bottles of SUPER COLD assorted sodas
- 6 cans San Pelligrino
- 1 loaf gluten free bread
- 1 bag gluten free crackers
- 1 Crunchy White Almond Butter
- 1 bag or raw Almonds
- 1 Grape Jelly
- Dirty Brand Potato chips
- 1 bag salyed kettle chips
- 1 box Mills wafers
- 1 Bunch bananas
- 5 fresh lemons
- Fresh Ginger Root
- Kettle, mugs, teaspoons, English Breakfast tea, Fresh Cream
- 1 regulat squuzed honey
- 1 Manuka Honey
- 1 full length mirror
- 1 toothbrush and toothpaste
- ! Framed picture of Carl Sagan
- Cetraphil spap bar and soap dish
- Cetaphil cleansing wipes
- Cetaphil cleansing lotion
- 1 box tissues

To purchase all this food I was given a staff car and driver. Believe it or not it took 3 days travelling around London to purchase all the Items. There was only 1 thing I could not purchase and that was a Framed Picture of Carl Sagan. Carl was an Ameican astronomer, cosmologist, author etc. I have no idea why they asked for this but I could not find it and nothing was mentioned

For one reason they did not require any hot food. But I know know why. The Rolling Stones arrived at Wembley at approximately 12pm on the day of a show. They rehearsed for up to a hour between 2-3pm. They they took themselves away and had a meal at I don't know where. They arrived back at Wembley at approximately 6pm, ready for the show at 8pm and were gone a maximun 10 minites after the show. I never got to meet or even saw them.

As I have said earlier I had to laminate and distribute Back Stage Passes but this was impossible. Even Mick Jagger needed a pass but there was no way I was being let in to give out passes.

I met the touring manager and he said he would distribute the passses. I am sure Harvey Goldsmith met the band but as later discovered later no one else at HGE.

I remember going into the dressing rooms after the show and I would say that 75% of the items requested were untouched.

Believe it or not they played 2 dates at Wembley and all the above items that were not used on day 1 had to be thrown away and replaced with new the next day.

I will end this section by saying two things:-

- The Rolling Stones put on two amazing shows
- What they requested in their rider was bordering on ridiculous

The rest of 1982 came and went with no shows. I managed to take a month off and travelled to India but that is a seperate story.

I returned to the office early in 1983. The place was buzzing and I could now wait to hear wehat was happening next.

I was called into an office and told by Andrew Zweck that David Bowie was touring later that year. Not only that but this was to be my biggest job so far. David was doing gigs for HGE at Wembley Arena, Birmingham NEC, Edinburgh, London Hammersmith Odeon and 3 nights at The National Bowl in Milton Keynes. My job as usual was to laminate passes and purchase the rider for 8 shows. As you will later find out it was not as hard a rider as The Stones but it involved a lot of travelling.

The Jam

The Jam were an English mod revival/punk rock band during the 1970s and early 1980s, which formed in 1972 at Sheerwater Secondary School

in Woking, in the county of Surrey. The band released 18 consecutive Top 40 singles in the United Kingdom, from their debut in 1977 to their break-up in December 1982, including four number one hits. As of 2007, "That's Entertainment" and "Just Who Is the 5 O'Clock Hero?" remain the best-selling import singles of all time in the UK.[4] They released one live album and six studio albums, the last of which, The Gift, hit number one on the UK Albums Chart. When the group disbanded in 1982, their first 15 singles were re-released and all placed within the top 100.[5]

While the Jam shared the "angry young man" outlook and fast tempo of the mid-1970s British punk rock movement, in contrast with it the band wore smartly tailored suits reminiscent of English pop-bands in the early 1960s and incorporated mainstream 1960s rock and R&B influences into its sound, particularly from the Who's work of that period and also drew influence from the work of the Kinks and the music of American Motown. This placed the act at the forefront of the 1970s–1980s nascent Mod Revival movement. With many of the band's lyrics about working class life,[6] Jam biographer Sean Egan commented that they "took social protest and cultural authenticity to the top of the charts."[7]

The band drew upon a variety of stylistic influences over the course of their career, including 1960s beat music, soul, rhythm and blues and psychedelic rock, as well as 1970s punk and new wave. The trio were known for their melodic pop songs, their distinctly English flavour and their mod image. The band launched the career of Paul Weller, who went on to form the Style Council and later his solo career. Weller wrote and sang most of the Jam's original compositions and played lead guitar, using a Rickenbacker 330. Bruce Foxton provided backing vocals and prominent basslines, which were the foundation of many of the band's songs, including the hits "Down in the Tube Station at Midnight", "The Eton Rifles", "Going Underground" and "Town Called Malice" mainly using a Rickenbacker 4001 or a Fender Precision Bass, as well as, on rare occasions, an Epiphone Rivoli.(WIKAPEDIA)

The next shows I was involved with were the Jam's farewll concets at Wembley Arena, which was for 3 nights. I should have told you this before but one of my jobs aside from obtaining the rider was to to laminate all the backstage passses and give the out to the crew. A backstage pass gave you access to food and drink but without a pass you got nothing. Now for Simon and Garfunkel most of the crew were american. They received their passes with grace and good cheer. The Jam crew were very different. I specifically remember on more than one occassion approaching a crew member after I was told who they were. The meeting went something like this.

"Hello are you ... ..."
"What the f**k do you want you c**t

"Well my name is Andrew and I have your backstage pass. As you know all the food and drink are backstage and you cannot access this without a pass. So when I say hello again in about an hours time, you will be more polite"

I would then walk away. I remember on one occasion a crew member apologised straight away and I gave him his pass. Another crew member threatened to punch me so I ran away. They couldn't chase me because they were ususaly busy with some task or other. Most of the crew accepted their fate and were more polite a second time around.

Now the rider for The Jam was different than Simon and Garfunkel. I must admit I have no idea what the S&G crew ate but I did not provide it. The Jam were not interested in any hot meals. There were three dressing rooms backstage and each dressing room had to have the following

48 Cans Of coke
12 Bottles Of Jamesons Irish Whisky
40 (yes 40) rounds of sandwiches made with different fillings and to include vegetarian
Six bottles of Red wine
Six Bottles White Wine
30 packets of assorted crisps
5 packs of Marlboro ciararettes
5 packs of Benson and Hedges cigarettes
packets John Player cigarettes
Table and chairs for 8

Now most of the above were easily obtainable from local supermarkets. I did have a problem getting the sanwiches, until I remembered, I daily went to a sandwich shop around the corner from work. I approached the owner and asked if he could provide 120 rounds of sandwiches in 3 boxes. He laughed and thought I was joking at first until I told him where I worked and who the sandwiches were for.

The sandwiches he produced were excellent. How do I know i hear you ask. Well bands always ask for a lot of food but it is rarely ever completely eaten. I took home enough sandwiches for the following week. As well as that because I placed such a huge order I got a reduction on my daily sandwich rate.

Before I continue let me tell you a story about what happened at an after show party for Simon and Garfunkel. The event was at a posh nightclub in London. All HGE staff had tickets. I arrived at about 7pm to join a short queue ready to gain entrance. In front of me was a famous female singer who had been in the business for over 40 years and was a household name. I will not mentuion her name but I will say would be recognised by most of he UK population if not the world.The problem was she did not have a ticket. The person on the door was very strict. No ticket no entrance. She proceeded to say

"Do you not know who I am?"

Everone in the queue knew her, but the doorman was strict, no ticket no entrance. I was in a dilema. Do I give her my ticket or do I enter and have a good time? What would you have done in that situation?

What happened was that I had a GREAT time. There were lots of famous people there that I saw. Unfortunately, when I started at HGE i was told that I would be meeting a lot of famous people but I was never ask them for anything not even an autograph. So yes there were a lot of famous people at the party but I approached none of them and spent my time with the rest of the HGE staff

David Bowie

David Robert Jones OAL (8 January 1947 – 10 January 2016), known professionally as David Bowie (/ˈboʊi/ BOH-ee),[1] was an English singer-songwriter and actor. A leading figure in the music industry, Bowie is regarded as one of the most influential musicians of the 20th century. He was acclaimed by critics and musicians, particularly for his innovative work during the 1970s. His career was marked by reinvention and visual presentation, with his music and stagecraft having a significant impact on popular music.

During his lifetime, his record sales, estimated at over 100 million records worldwide, made him one of the best-selling music artists of all time. In the UK, he was awarded ten platinum album certifications, eleven gold and eight silver, and released eleven number-one albums. In the US, he received five platinum and nine gold certifications. He was inducted into the Rock and Roll Hall of Fame in 1996. Rolling Stone placed him among its list of the 100 Greatest Artists of All Time and named him the "Greatest Rock Star Ever" following his death in 2016.

Born in Brixton, South London, Bowie developed an interest in music as a child. He studied art, music and design before embarking on a professional career as a musician in 1963. "Space Oddity", released in 1969, was his first top-five entry on the UK Singles Chart. After a period of experimentation, he re-emerged in 1972 during the glam rock era with his flamboyant and androgynous alter ego Ziggy Stardust. The character was spearheaded by the success of Bowie's single "Starman" and album The Rise and Fall of Ziggy Stardust and the Spiders from Mars, which won him widespread popularity. In 1975, Bowie's style shifted towards a sound he characterised as "plastic soul", initially alienating many of his UK fans but garnering him his first major US crossover success with the number-one single "Fame" and the album Young Americans. In 1976, Bowie starred in the cult film The Man Who Fell to Earth, directed by Nicolas Roeg, and released Station to Station. In 1977, he further confounded expectations with the electronic-inflected album Low, the first of three collaborations with Brian Eno that came to be known as the "Berlin Trilogy". "Heroes" (1977) and Lodger (1979) followed; each album reached the UK top five and received lasting critical praise.

After uneven commercial success in the late 1970s, Bowie had UK number ones with the 1980 single "Ashes to Ashes", its album Scary Monsters (and Super Creeps), and "Under Pressure", a 1981 collaboration with Queen. He reached his commercial peak in 1983 with Let's Dance; its title track topped both the UK and US charts. Throughout the 1990s and 2000s, Bowie continued to experiment with musical styles, including industrial and jungle. He also continued acting; his roles included Major Jack Celliers in Merry Christmas, Mr. Lawrence (1983), Jareth the Goblin King in Labyrinth (1986), Pontius Pilate in The Last Temptation of Christ (1988), and Nikola Tesla in The Prestige (2006), among other film and television appearances and cameos. He stopped touring after 2004 and his last live performance was at a charity event in 2006. In 2013, Bowie returned from a decade-long recording hiatus with The Next Day. He remained musically active until his death of liver cancer at his home in New York City, two days after his 69th birthday and the release of his final album, Blackstar(WIKAPEDIA)

Moving back to the office, It was not until February 1983 that I was told that the next shows would be. These shows were to be the highlight of my time at HGE.

Andwer Zweck sat me down and told me that David Bowie was touring that year and that HGE were promoting his UK Shows .

I was to be responsible once again for laminating and giving out backstage passes and for getting the food for the rider. BUT unlike Simon and Garfunkel this was not for just one show but for nine.

The shows were at

2-4 June Wembley Arena
5-6 June Birmingham NEC
28 June Edinburgh
30 June Hammersmith Odeon, London
1-3 July Milton Keynes Bowl.

I received the David Bowie rider two weeks before the Wembley shows. Although not as extensive as the Rolling Stones rider it was quite detailed. I kept these riders and you can see them below.

All these items above were needed new for each concert. Most of these items were not a problem and were supplied as requested at each venue. There is however one item not on the rider, which I subequantly found out later. On talking to the tour manager I was told that David's favourite dish was Sushi.

While he was at Wembley he went out to eat as he did at all other shows. It wasn't until we got to the Milton Keynes Bowl that problems arose. The Milton Keynes Bowl is a 65,000 capacity venue first built in 1979. Quite a few stars have appeared here in the past. These include Queen, Simple Minds, Michael Jackon, Take That and the Foo Fighters.

I was at all the above except Michael Jackson. One other show they put on in 1982 was very special to me. As you might have realised I was a Genesis fan. Lots of people know Genesis was fronted by Phil Colins, but not a lot of people didn't know that Genesis front man from 1969 to 1975 was Peter Gabriel.

The show at MK Bowl on Saturday 2 October 1982 was to be the first ond only reunion with Peter Gabriel. There were thousands of Genesis fans from all over the world. Peter arrived on stage in a coffin which he arose from to play all their old hits. It was a woneful day never to be repeated or forgotten. Everybody loved it. The only problem, it rained all day.

OK back to Bowie at the MK Bowl. As i said earlir Bowie liked Sushi to be served at every show when he was not eating out. Now in 1982 there were not many restaurants that served sushi in Milton Keynes. I therefore had to ring up a restaurant in London, travel down bytrain, go to the restaurant where they had prepard the Shushi and packed it in Ice which I them took back to Milton Keynes.

The major thing that was different from the Rolling Stones was that I got to meet David briefly at every show. I would never say we were friends but he seemed to appreciate all that I did for him. On the last night at MK Bowl he even shook my hand. I haven't washed it since.

One more storyaout the Bowie tour. I was currently living with my parents in Leighton Buzzard which is half an hour from Milton Keynes. Most days i travelled up and down to London by train. However for the fist MK show on 1 July I was amazed to be offered a place on the helicopter that took David to London.

Davie Bowie, myself and four others flew in the helicopter from London to Milton Keynes. I will always remeber landing at the helipad just putside MK Bowl. Hunderds of fans surrounded the pad and were cheering. I have never felt so special in my life.

OK finally one more point about David Bowe. Unlike the Rolling Stones who saw themselves as superstars, David was just a normal man. I will never forget seeing him at the concert at Hammersmith Odeon backstage before going on. He actually seemed quite nervous and he was wringing his hands. However, once he was on stage he was the true professional.

This tour was to be my highlight of working for Harvey Goldsmith and the Bowie tour could in my mind never be beaten. Therefore, in November 1983 I handed in my notice and left HGE. There was a very small party on my last day and I received £100

Live Aid

Live Aid was a benefit concert held on Saturday 13 July 1985, as well as a music-based fundraising initiative. The original event was organised by Bob Geldof and Midge Ure to raise funds for relief of the 1983–1985 famine in Ethiopia. Billed as the "global jukebox", the event was held simultaneously at Wembley Stadium in London, UK, attended by about 72,000 people and John F. Kennedy Stadium in Philadelphia, US, attended by 89,484 people. [1][2]

On the same day, concerts inspired by the initiative were held in other countries, such as the Soviet Union, Canada, Japan, Yugoslavia, Austria, Australia and West Germany. It was one of the largest satellite link-ups and television broadcasts of all time; an estimated audience of 1.9 billion, in 150 nations, watched the live broadcast, nearly 40 percent of the world population. [3][4]

The impact of Live Aid on famine relief has been debated for years. One aid relief worker stated that following the publicity generated by the concert, "humanitarian concern is now at the centre of foreign policy" for western governments.[5] Geldof has said, "We took an issue that was nowhere on the political agenda and, through the lingua franca of the planet – which is not English but rock 'n' roll – we were able to address the intellectual absurdity and the moral repulsion of people dying of want in a world of surplus."[6] In another interview he stated that Live Aid "created something permanent and self-sustaining" but also asked why Africa is getting poorer.[5] The organisers of Live Aid tried to run aid efforts directly, channelling millions of pounds to NGOs in Ethiopia. It has been alleged that much of this went to the Ethiopian government of Mengistu Haile Mariam – a regime the UK Prime Minister Margaret Thatcher opposed[7] – and it is also alleged some funds were spent on guns.[5][8] The BBC stated in 2010 there was no evidence money had been diverted,[9] while the former British Ambassador to Ethiopia, Brian Barder, states, "the diversion of aid related only to the tiny proportion that was supplied by some NGOs to rebel-held areas."[10] Believe it or not in February 1985 I received an unexpected phone call from Andrew Zweck. He had a proposition for me and asked to to come to the HGE offices in London.(WIKAPEDIA)

The following week up I went up to see him.

He told me the following story.

In November Band Aid was formed. Band Aid was a charity supergroup featuring mainly British and Irish musicians and recording artists. [1][2][3] It was founded in 1984 by Bob Geldof and Midge Ure to raise money for anti-famine efforts in Ethiopia by releasing the song "Do

They Know It's Christmas?" for the Christmas market that year. On 25 November 1984, the song was recorded at Sarm West Studios in Notting Hill, London, and was released in the UK on Monday 3 December. [4][5] The single surpassed the hopes of the producers to become the Christmas number one on that release.

I knew all about Band Aid becausde it had been such a success and I had seen it all happen in television.

What I did not expect was what followed. Harvey along with Bob Geldof and Midge ure were planning on raising more money than Band aid by putting on two concerts at Wembley Stadium and JFK Stadium in Phiadelphia. Bill Graham was to be the American promoter

Andrew asked me because of my experience working with David Bowie whether I would work as his assistant for Live Aid. I obviously agreed but it was not until the following weeks that I found out just how big Live Aid was going to be. Over the next week artists such Elton John, Queen, Madonna, Santana, Run DMC, Sade, Sting, Bryan Adams, the Beach Boys, Mick Jagger, David Bowie, Queen, Duran Duran, U2, the Who, Tom Petty, Neil Young, and Eric Clapton were all to appear at Wembley Staduim on Saturday 13 July.

I later found out the acts to appear in America. These included Tina Turner, Mick Jagger, Eric Clapton, Crosby, Stills, Nash and Young, The Beach Boys, Hall and Oates, Bob Dylan and Phil Collins. Collins performed in Philadelphia after performing at Wembley earlier in the day.

Also very unexpectedly on the day was to by the first Reunion by Led Zeppelin. Unfortunately, they performed badly that day. Led Zeppelin decided to reunite for the first time since drummer John Bonham's death. There were many factors that made the performance a train wreck. Singer Robert Plant's voice was sore from playing three solo shows in the nights before Live Aid, guitarist Jimmy Page was handed a guitar that hadn't been tuned properly, and Phil Collins was added as a second drummer at the last minute and was noticeably unfamiliar with the material.

To their credit, Zeppelin bassist/keyboardist John Paul Jones and fill-in drummer Tony Thompson (Chic/The Power Station) both played solidly. Most of the audience probably didn't initially notice the flaws in the performance. But Jimmy Page noticed enough to later excludes Led Zeppelin's performance from the Live Aid DVD set released in 2004. Unfortunately for Zeppelin that same year a new internet video service called YouTube made the performance viewable to anyone with a computer and an internet connection.

OK back to Wembley. I was to meet David Bowie and Andrew Zweck at the offices in Wembley Stadium. My job was to follow David around and to ensure all requests were met.

It was the easiest job I ever had. After meeting with Andrew and David I was to ensure David made in to the Royal Box at 11.45 before the show started. I met up with David outside the Royal box and gave him his ticket

I, obviously had no ticket so I was to meet David outside the Royal box at 11.55.

This I did and it was then that he told me I was not needed until his performance at 6pm.

I spent.my time both backstage at Live Aid and milling with the crowd. I spent a lot of my time backstage where the Hard Rock cafe were providing free drinks and meals for performers etc. I was lucky enough to have a pass which gave me these things.

It was an amazing time. While in the Hard Rock cafe superstars came and went just like normal people. In my time there I saw Bono, Brian May and Freddie Mercury all eating burgers and enjoying themselves. Unfortunately, my duty was to look after David Bowie but I was not allowed to approach any other artist.

All these famous people eating burgers feet away from me and I could do nothing.

My most famous memory was seeing Freddie Mercury eating with Phil Collins.

Finally, I ensured I met David Bowie backstage and he went onto to perform hs show. Later in the evening, following David Bowie's set, a video shot by the Canadian Broadcasting Corporation was shown to the audiences in London and Philadelphia, as well as on televisions around the world, showing starving and diseased Ethiopian children set to "Drive" by The CarsThe rate of donations became faster in the immediate aftermath of the video. Geldof had previously refused to allow the video to be shown, due to time constraints, and had only relented when Bowie offered to drop the song "Five Years" from his set as a trade-off.

After his set my only job was to ensure David made it to the stage for the finale. I must admit the finale was a bit of a experience for me. I had arranged to meet David at 10.30 backstage but come 10.30 there were a large amont of stars there and I coud not find him.

Luckily before they started singing, I saw him among the crowd. The final song was sung and 72,000 people including myself made their way home.

Friars Aylesbury

Friars Aylesbury is a music club that runs in Aylesbury, Buckinghamshire, England.[1] It opened in 1969 but closed down twice, once in 1970 for a period of nine months and again in 1984 for a period of twenty-five years. Friars Aylesbury reopened in June 2009 to tie in with its fortieth anniversary.[2]

Friars Aylesbury ran as a music club in the market town of Aylesbury in Buckinghamshire between 1969 and 1984 in three distinct phases denoted by the venue in the town. Over these fifteen years, there were various trials and tribulations which saw Friars close to bankruptcy more than once but it survived and presented the best artists of its day and is acknowledged as being heavily responsible for the subsequent success of such artists as David Bowie, Genesis, Wishbone Ash, Mott the Hoople, Cockney Rebel, Sailor, Stackridge, Stiff Little Fingers and more. Fans and artists loved the club, not least because of the atmosphere and the fact they were treated well by people who were genuine music enthusiasts.(WIKAPEDIA)

I took a month off before contacting a person I had met at the Friars Rock venue in Aylesbury.

The chap was called David Stopps and he initially founded Friars Aylesbury back in 1969 through to 1985

The venue ran in three different locations during this time. Some amazing artists had appeared at the venue including Queen who appeared there in their early days. Believe it or not the price for the Queen concert was only 75p

Other acts included David Bowie who unveiled his Ziggy Stardust persona on the Aylesbuy audience and many press including US journalists. David first played Friars in 1971 to se if he could cut it playing live. He needn'thave worried. Not only did he go down a storm that night but he gave Aylesbury the world debut of Hunky Dory which ast the time had not been released.

After the gig in the Friars dressing room he said to other band members "This was great tonight. Lets form a band and go out and do it properly"

So Friars Aylesbury and David Bowie had a great history, so when David died in 2016, Friars Aylesbury set up a fundraising page and managed to raise £100,000 toward a statue of Bowie. The statue sings Bowie sings every hour on the hour and standsin the Market Square which Bowie referenced Iin Five Years, the opening tack of The Rise and Fall of Ziggy Stardust and the Spiders from Mars album.

While working with David at Friars I was responsible for helping out with press releases and distributing posters throughtout the town. I also had to distribute to many venues in the Buckinghamshire region

I was only at Friars for two events. On Saturday November 5th The Alarm played Friars. Not being a huge fan I obviously attended the gig but it was not until the next concert that my skills were in demand.

The concert was to be The Eurythmics. The date was Monday October 31st and unusual day for a concert. This was billed initially as a secret gig, Friars being much smaller than other venues on the tour, but it sold out well in advance.

Annie Lennox, Dave Stewart and the rest of the band arrived at approximately midday. The soon settled into their soundcheck which finished at 3pm.

For the remaing hours before the show we mainly enjoyed a meal and drinks in the theatre. This was interesting because Annie Lennox was a vegetarian as so all the food was also.

It was interesting to be eating food with a major star. It was just like a family meal.

The concert itself was amazing. People were standing everywhere and it was my job to stand between the stage and crowd to stop people climbing onto the stage. This never happened but I had a great view of the band

My life outside music

Although I had fun working for David Stopps at Friars the money was not great and so I decided it was time I got a proper job. I wracked my brain and decided I wanted to work with people with learning disabilities. I secured a job as a Support Worker for MacIntyre Care at Westoning in Bedfirdshure and worked.

I worked at Macintyre for approximately 8 years as a support worker. However in 1991 I was approached by the CEO. They had somehow found out about my previous history and wanted to put on a concert to raise funds. The venue was going to be in Milton Keynes and they wanted a big name to headline.

Despite my experiance and working with a large Leighton Buzzard company no big names came forward. I cannot remember how it happened but we moved to put on a Laser and Firewaok show in Westoning Manor Grounds.

This was quite easy to orgasnise. There was no rider. The organisation, Performing Arts, turned up using a large lorry as a stage. Fireworks and Lasers were positioned around the site. My main job was to sell tickets.

On the day of the event over 2000 people turned up to watch what was a fantastic show. The music from the stage was very clear, the fireworks were great and the lasers shone staggering images on surrounding trees. Overall the event was a success, with money being raised for MacIntyre

Unforunately, after the show it was back to work as normal

I was placed to work in a different home that I had worked in previously and felt resentment from other staff. I only stayed for about a year before moving to another organisation, Freemantle Care. At Freemantle I was again a support worker but after working there for a couple of years I was approached by a senior manager and asked if I wanted to manage a different home. This was totally out of the blue and I said yes.

The home was called Bracken House in Bedfordshire. I was a very large house with a total of 11 clients, 5 upstairs and 6 downstairs. I was to manage downstairs and a separate manager was to manage upstairs. From there I moved to a position of Deputy Manager at Shakespeare Way in Aylesbury. We had such fun on those holidays that one day I found her address and made an impromptu visit. She was a bit surprised to see me but invited me in. Over two years later I moved into her studio flat before we moved into my house in Browns Wood, Milton Keynes. Six years later we bought the house were are living in today, 111 Victoria Street, Wolverton, Milton Keynes

After a few years we took on a dog called Merlot. Merliot lived until the ripe old age of 17 befre we sadly had to have her out down. She was soon replaced by Orinoco, a sllightly mad chocolate labrador who is with us to this day

Now to be honest with you I was not a very good manager. I had no experience and was resented by a number of staff, who having worked there a number of years they felt that they shoud have been offered the manager job, not some outsider.

I managed to muddle through. At the same time I was teaching Equality and Diversity couses at the local colleague in Milton Keynes. This was something I was good at and enjoyed. Fremantle soon found out I was working for the college as well as them and I was told to make a choice. Either work full time at Freemantle or the college but not both.

It didnt take long for me to decide. I had a meeting with the college and they offered me a post on the spot.

Very soon I was working a four day week teaching adults with learning disabilities English, Maths and Drama.

Every Tuesday, I was to work in Milton Keynes prison teaching inmated. This job was interesting and very enjoyable but there were a few negative pints.

Firstly, getting into the prison as a slight headache. You were thoroughly frisked and inspected each time yont in, rightfully so. However, I found myself teaching category A prisoners. Now category A prisoners are those that would pose the most threat to the public, the police or national security should they escape. Security conditions in category A prisons are designed to make escape impossible for these prisoners.

I was told that a lot of these prisoners were in for life (20 years) and had no real need or want for education. I taught a group of about 8 and got to know them quite well. They weren't interested in learning anything so we spent the time I was there just chatting. Chatting basically about what they had seen on television that week. This is basically all they had to talk about. Aside from an hours education they were released from there cells for one hours excercise a day.

I also worked on the same day on the sex offenders unit. Here the prisoners had more freedom and liked to enterain themselves by playing music and taking. There were an intersting bunch but with all prisoners I had to forget why they were inside. This often became sligtly difficult. Each prisoner had on the wall a card with full details of their crime. I only read one before deciding my job in prison was to educate and not think about previous crimes committed. I only worked there a year before getting a full 5 day week at college.

In 2009 I had to leave college. I was suffering from depression. The doctors put me on anti-depressants which for some reason ouy me on a high. I could no longer teach while in such a state. I left the college and took a year trying to ger free of the dugs that I had stopped taking.

After the year I worked for a variety of work agencies which brings me right up to date. I am currently working (but furloughed during lockdown) for two companies. SEP Events and Forward Security. For SEP I work a lot and Silverstne and Cheltenham and other events. At Forward I work for mainly football teams including MK Dons, QPR, Watford and Wembley. OK that brings me up to date lets get back to the music.

Global Festival

Milton Keynes Global Festival started in 1986 and was held at the Willen Mini Bowl. Over the next 10 years it moved to a variety of locations until in 1993, it moved to Capbell Park. This is when I joined the committee.

The festival was run from Saturday to Sunday. The Sunday was based mainly with local singing and dance bands, wheras the Sunday hosted national acts. These included The Oyseer Band, Judy Tzuke and a variey of bands from arouind the world. The festival was free to all as we received a grant from the local council. I was the stage manager from 1990 to 1993

Open University

From about 1995 to 2005 I also helped to promote concerts at Milton Keynes Open Univesity. The concerts ran with the theme of One World and we managed to secure performances from a varity of audiences. The final performance was by Tom Robinson

Acoustic Festival

In 2009 I was invited to work at the Acoustic Festival near Stoke. I was to receive a free ticket for the event but in return I had to collect litter.

I was collecting litter one day when I soon realised there were no comperes introducing the bands. I approached one of the owners and asked if I could compere. I ended up compareing four stages.

Loads of amazing acts appeared at the Acoustic Festival and I am going to tell you a couple of stories.

One day Fish ex from Marillion arrived and I introduced myself. He invited me into his large Winebego where I proceeded to drink a bottle of wine. Things were going well until it came time to introduce Fish on the stage. In my alcoholic state I could not remember who was next on stage. Lucking I saw Fisn in the background and remembered. From that day until today I never drink when I am working.

Another story concerns Joan Armatrading. She was introduced and went on to perform well on stage. The only thing slightly wrong was thst she didn't introduce her songs on stage.

She was also awarded a "Lifetime Achievemeny Award" but refused to receive the trophy on stage. Very unusual behaviour from a popular singer. Maybe she was just having a bad day.

I have worked at the Acoustic festival every year from 2009 to the present day. I am alway the compere and as well as receiving a free ticket I currently also get fed.

My camping years are behind me and for the last 6 years I have stayed in a local B&B. I really enjoy The Acoustic Festival. I currently also help the promoter choosing bands. It ever you find yourselves with nothing to do I urge you go to The Acoustic Festival. Its currently held at Uttoxetrer Racecouse and tickets for the weekend are only £99 which is amazing value for a festival.

Togfest

TOGFEST is an all music festival at the historic Bradwell Abbey in the heart of Milton Keynes. We showcase great original music that you may have not seen before. We will be back in 2022.

Togfest was originally founded to celebrate the 10th Birthday party of local folk rock legends Togmor. However, they worked out you can have a birthday party every year and it's been going from strength to strength ever since. Way back in 1979 as you have read earlier I went to see Peter Gabriel and Genesis at Friars Aylesbury. I went with a chap called Ian Rowe. I met Ian early in 1979 at a party at a friends house. We had never met before but soon found we had a lot in common. Ian was learning to play the guitar and I vividly remember meeting him at his house on Friday evenings where he woud practice. Being a non musician I played the tambourine.

Move onto to 1988 and Ian formed a band balled Togmor with friend Gavin Bunker who persuaded Ian to start something folky but with drums (Gavin was a drummer and fan of Fairport Convention drummer, Dave Mattocks). The band was formed with John Gibbons on electric guitar, Kevin Cranfield on bass and Jonathan Ginn on Fiddle duty.

In 1998 Ian started the festival Togfest at Bradwell Abbey in Milton Keynes. I was a regular at Togfest until in 1979 I asked if I could compere one of the stages. This I did and have done until the present day. One big memory was in 2018 when Togmor celebrated their 20th anniversary. I was compere and lots of old faces including Gavin Bunker turned up to what was a greast evening of music and memories

Woburn Sands Festival

In 1995 I was managing a band called Inlakesh. Inlakesh came from Milton Keynes, UK, who work tirelessly on creating succulent, ear pleasing yet hard hitting grooves, delivering distinctive albeit confusingly intricate Spanish scale to Arabian influenced melodies and evoking rhythmical senses with punctuated pauses and timely grabs to create shock and awe.

I managed to get Inlakesh booked into the Woburn Sands Festival in 1995. The band played well and i got chatting to the organiser Gill Brooke. As I introduced In lakesh I asked if they needed a compere for the following year. My offer was greatfully accepted and I have been compere and stage manager ever since.

We were luck in 2001 because the festival as able to be held in August. However, there was a difference. Instead of a one day festival it was to be two days and instead of one stage we had two stages in the regular field as well as using a local pub as a second venue

Wolverton Festival

My home town of Wolverton held a mini festival every year in the local shopping square. I didnt feel that this was the right place for a festival so i rarely went along.

I was not until 2014 that I approach the local council with an idea. I wanted to put on a festival at one of the large parks in Wolverton. Believe it or not the council were having the same idea and I soon found myself once again on the committee.

The festival has been running ever since and is a popular event in the Wolverton calender.

So there we have it. In the past 40 years I have promoted concerts and festivals, managed bands, stage managed and compered a lot of festivals.